Anfisa Plants a Rock

by Svetlana Perry

"Anfisa Plants A Rock"
A Gentle Nature Story for Curious Kids
Anfisa's Garden Adventures Series
Book 1

Hello!
Look at Anfisa.

Yes — she is a monkey.

She loves children.

She loves nature.

She loves finding
surprises
in the garden.

ah, ah, ah, ah!
I help Anfisa and the children in the garden.

Today Anfisa and the children
are in the garden.

They have their
little shovels.

They are digging,
digging, digging.

"Anfisa, what are you doing?"

Anfisa looks up and smiles.

In her hand is... an acorn!

Brown, smooth,
and round.

"Oh! An acorn," I say.
"That's a seed!
Let's plant it here."
We dig a small hole.
The acorn goes in.
Plop!
We cover it gently.
OAK

"What's next, Anfisa?"
Ah, ah, ah, ah!
Anfisa holds up...
a rock?!
OAK

"Well… okay! Let's see
what happens."

We dig another hole.
We plant the rock.
We pat the soil.

OAK
ROCK

Anfisa grabs a bucket with water.
"You like watering, don't you?"
Water splashes
everywhere —

Ah, ah, ah, ah!
OAK
ROCK
on the acorn, on the rock,
on Anfisa's feet!

Every morning, Anfisa runs
outside.

She checks the acorn.
She checks the rock.
She waters both carefully.

One sunny morning Anfisa
discovers...

...a tall
green
sprout
growing
from the
soil!

"Did your rock grow?"
OAK
ROCK

Anfisa waits.
She wiggles her eyebrows.
Nothing.
Rocks don't grow.

Only things with life in them
can grow.

Anfisa thinks.

Then she smiles.

She runs back with...
a coconut!

"That's a seed," I say.
"It can grow."
Ah, ah, oh...!
PALM
OAK
ROCK

Song time!

(it fits the tune of
"The Wheels on the Bus")

Stanza 1

I plant a rock and a seed — dig, dig, dig
I water them gently — whoosh, whoosh, whoosh
I plant a rock and a seed — dig, dig, dig
I am an explorer!

Stanza 2

The seed has life, it will sprout — grow, grow, grow
The rock has none, it stays there — still, still, still
The seed has life, it will sprout — grow, grow, grow
What a miracle!

Why did the acorn grow but the rock didn't?
Seeds come from living plants. Inside every seed is a tiny baby plant, curled up and waiting to grow. When a seed gets soil, water, air, and sunlight, it wakes up and begins to sprout! A rock is different. Rocks are not alive, so they cannot grow roots, leaves, or branches. But rocks still play an important part in nature: they help hold soil in place, make homes for insects, and provide minerals for plants to grow!

Seeds grow.

Rocks stay.

Both belong in the wonderful world of the garden.

Try this!

Plant two things:
A seed and a rock

You will need:
One seed (an acorn, a bean, or a pea works great!)
A cup (poke a hole in the bottom for extra water to drip out)
or a flower pot
Some soil
Water

Fill your cup with soil.
Make a tiny hole with your finger.
Drop your seed and a rock inside.
Cover it gently with soil.
Give it a small drink of water.
Place it somewhere sunny.
Check your seed each day.
Does the soil feel dry? Water it gently.
When you see a green sprout... say,

"Hello, little plant!"

Anfisa's Garden Adventures 

follows Anfisa, the little monkey, a curious little friend who loves children, gardens, and exploring the wonders of nature.

Each story in the series blends:
- Real-life outdoor adventures
- Early science and nature discoveries
- Emotional learning
- Songs and rhymes
- Simple, hands-on garden activities

Through gentle humor and wonder-filled exploration, Anfisa helps young readers notice hidden life in the soil, the beauty of growing things, and the joy of caring for our planet.

Perfect for ages 3–6, these stories spark imagination, curiosity, and gratitude—
one small adventure at a time.

About the author

Svetlana Perry is a country girl with a PhD who teaches gardening to preschoolers.

She believes in simple joys, grateful living, and the miracle of growing things with young children.

Svetlana treasures her family, her church, and all her friends—big and small.

She hopes her stories inspire little readers to wonder, explore, and care for our amazing planet.

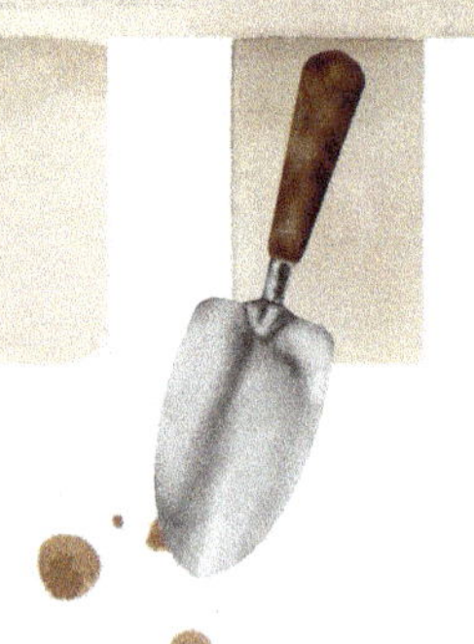